AMAZING TRAINS

High-Speed Trains

by Christina Leighton

BLASTOFF! READERS

BELLWETHER MEDIA · MINNEAPOLIS, MN

Note to Librarians, Teachers, and Parents:

Blastoff! Readers are carefully developed by literacy experts and combine standards-based content with developmentally appropriate text.

Level 1 provides the most support through repetition of high-frequency words, light text, predictable sentence patterns, and strong visual support.

Level 2 offers early readers a bit more challenge through varied simple sentences, increased text load, and less repetition of high-frequency words.

Level 3 advances early-fluent readers toward fluency through increased text and concept load, less reliance on visuals, longer sentences, and more literary language.

Level 4 builds reading stamina by providing more text per page, increased use of punctuation, greater variation in sentence patterns, and increasingly challenging vocabulary.

Level 5 encourages children to move from "learning to read" to "reading to learn" by providing even more text, varied writing styles, and less familiar topics.

Whichever book is right for your reader, Blastoff! Readers are the perfect books to build confidence and encourage a love of reading that will last a lifetime!

This edition first published in 2018 by Bellwether Media, Inc.

No part of this publication may be reproduced in whole or in part without written permission of the publisher. For information regarding permission, write to Bellwether Media, Inc., Attention: Permissions Department, 5357 Penn Avenue South, Minneapolis, MN 55419.

Library of Congress Cataloging-in-Publication Data

Names: Leighton, Christina, author.
Title: High-speed Trains / by Christina Leighton.
Description: Minneapolis, MN : Bellwether Media, Inc., [2018] | Series:
    Blastoff! Readers: Amazing Trains | Includes bibliographical references
    and index. | Audience: Age 5-8. | Audience: Grade K to 3.
Identifiers: LCCN 2016052934 (print) | LCCN 2017010228 (ebook) | ISBN
    9781626176713 (hardcover : alk. paper) | ISBN 9781681034010 (ebook)
Subjects: LCSH: High speed trains–Juvenile literature.
Classification: LCC TF1455 .L45 2018 (print) | LCC TF1455 (ebook) | DDC
    625.2/3–dc23
LC record available at https://lccn.loc.gov/2016052934

Editor: Nathan Sommer   Designer: Lois Stanfield

Printed in the United States of America, North Mankato, MN.

Table of Contents

WHAT ARE HIGH-SPEED TRAINS?

High-speed trains go very fast. They carry **passengers** to different places.

They stop often
to let people on
and off.

出站口
Ex

7

BUILT FOR SPEED

High-speed trains are also called **bullet** trains. They are shaped like bullets for speed.

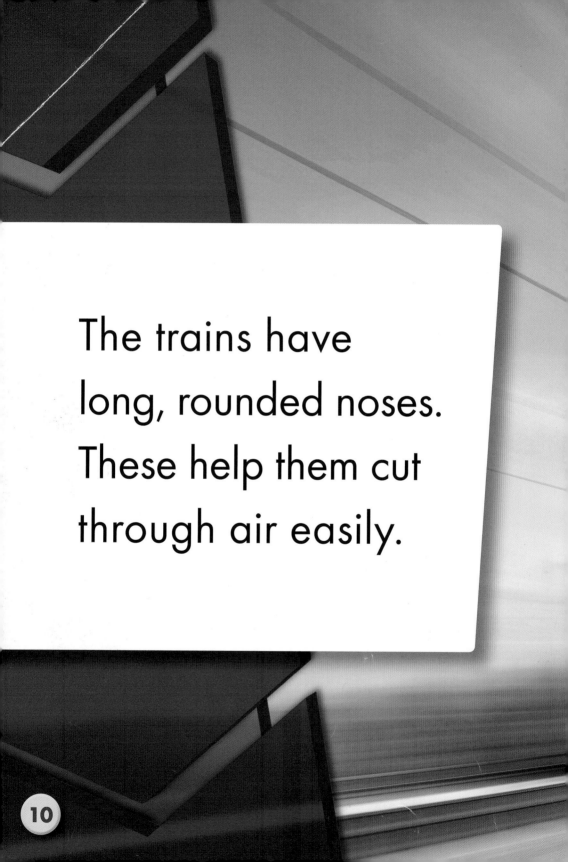

The trains have long, rounded noses. These help them cut through air easily.

HOW FAST?

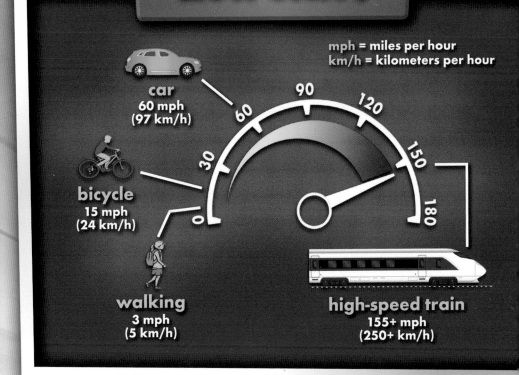

mph = miles per hour
km/h = kilometers per hour

car
60 mph
(97 km/h)

bicycle
15 mph
(24 km/h)

walking
3 mph
(5 km/h)

high-speed train
155+ mph
(250+ km/h)

nose

High-speed trains are made up of many **cars**. They carry millions of people every day!

cars

These trains can move backward and forward. Some float over **magnetic tracks**.

magnetic tracks

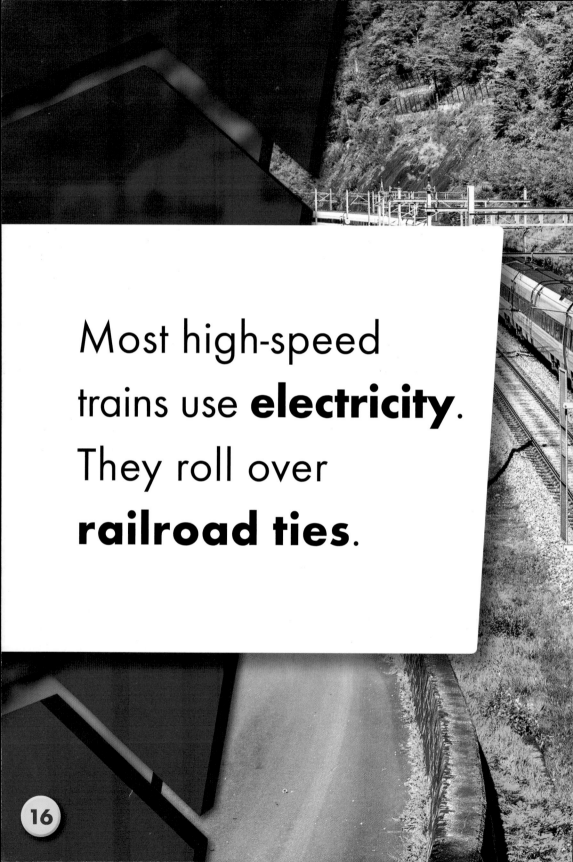

Most high-speed trains use **electricity**. They roll over **railroad ties**.

electricity

railroad ties

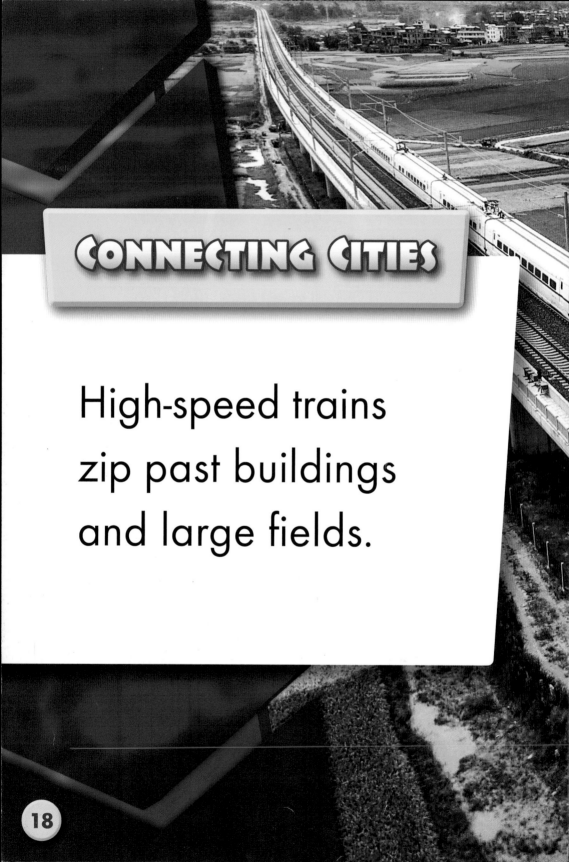

CONNECTING CITIES

High-speed trains zip past buildings and large fields.

These trains help connect cities. They make traveling fast for passengers!

Glossary

bullet

a long, rounded piece of metal fired from a gun

magnetic tracks

sets of tracks that use magnets to move trains

cars

vehicles pulled by a train

passengers

people who ride a vehicle to get from one place to another

electricity

a form of energy that gives power

railroad ties

beams that are underneath the rails to support them

To Learn More

AT THE LIBRARY

Clapper, Nikki Bruno. *High-Speed Trains.*
North Mankato, Minn.: Capstone Press, 2016.

Glaser, Rebecca Stromstad. *Trains.*
Minneapolis, Minn.: Jump!, 2013.

Riggs, Kate. *Bullet Trains.* Mankato, Minn.:
Creative Education, 2015.

ON THE WEB

Learning more about
high-speed trains is as
easy as 1, 2, 3.

1. Go to www.factsurfer.com.

2. Enter "high-speed trains" into the
   search box.

3. Click the "Surf" button and you will see a
   list of related web sites.

With factsurfer.com, finding more information
is just a click away.

Index

The images in this book are reproduced through the courtesy of: Serjio74, front cover; Scanrail1, pp. 2-3; Nicholashan, pp. 4-5; nattapan72, pp. 6-7; Xinhua/ Alamy, pp. 8-9; Ortodox, pp. 10-11; Mlap Studio, p. 11 (speedometer); autovector, p. 11 (train); taoty, p. 11 (car); NiklsN, p. 11 (bicycle); Vector Draco, p. 11 (pedestrian); Dmitry Mizintsev, pp. 12-13; cyo bo, pp. 14-15; Leonid Andronov, pp. 16-17; Wei Wanzhong Xinhua News Agency/ Newscom, pp. 18-19, 22 (bottom right); Wu Jibin Xinhua News Agency/ Newscom, pp. 20-21; Guy J. Sagi, p. 22 (top left); r.nagy, p. 22 (top right); scanrail, p. 22 (center left); Vincent St. Thomas, p. 22 (center right); Didier ZYLBERYNG/ Alamy, p. 22 (bottom left).